# KIDS ON EARTH

*Wildlife Adventures – Explore The World*
*Blue Footed Booby - Ecuador*

Sensei Paul David

# Copyright Page

Kids On Earth: Wildlife Adventures - Explore The World

Blue Footed Booby - Ecuador

by Sensei Paul David,

Copyright © 2023.

All rights reserved.

978-1-77848-187-1 KoE_WildLife_Amazon_PaperbackBook_ecuador_blue footed booby

978-1-77848-186-4 KoE_WildLife_Amazon_eBook_ecuador_blue footed booby

978-1-77848-423-0 KoE_Wildlife_Ingram_Paperbackbook_BlueFootedBoobyBird

This book is not authorized for free distribution copying.

www.senseipublishing.com

@senseipublishing
#senseipublishing

## Synopsis

This book is an exploration of the unique, fun facts about the Blue-Footed Booby in Ecuador. It provides an introduction to the bird, and then dives into facts about its diet, habitat, behaviors, and more. It also includes information about their courtship rituals and how long they can live in the wild and in captivity. It finishes with a conclusion about how to spot them in their natural habitat.

# Get Our FREE Books Now!

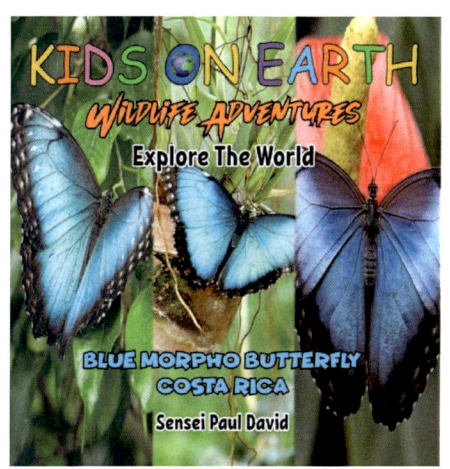

kidsonearth.life

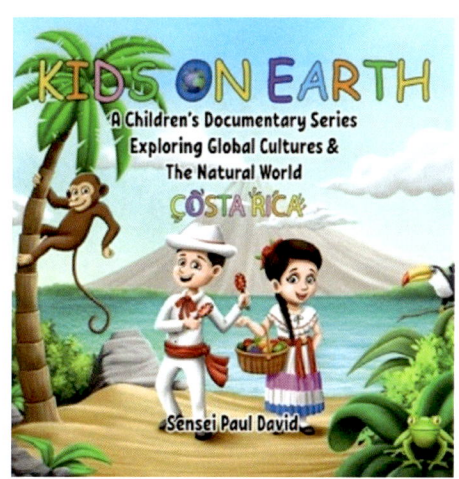

kidsonearth.world

# Click Below for Another Book In Each Series

senseipublishing.com/KoE_SERIES

senseipublishing.com/KoE_Wildlife_SERIES

## KoE En Español

senseipublishing.com/KoE_SERIES_SPANISH

www.senseipublishing.com

# Join Our Publishing Journey!

If you would like to receive FUTURE FREE BOOKS and get to know us better, please click www.senseipublishing.com and join our newsletter by entering your email address in the pop-up box.

**Follow Our Blog: senseipauldavid.ca**

Follow/Like/Subscribe: Facebook, Instagram, YouTube: @senseipublishing

Scan the QR Code with your phone or tablet to follow us on social media:

Like / Subscribe / Follow

# Introduction

Welcome to the wonderful world of the Blue-Footed Booby in Ecuador! This book is packed full of fun and interesting facts about these fascinating birds. You'll learn about their diet, habitat, and behaviors, as well as some of the unique things that make them so special. So let's get started!

Blue-footed boobies are tropical seabirds found along the coast of Ecuador.

They have bright blue feet, beaks, and facial markings.

Their wingspan can reach up to three feet in length.

They are excellent swimmers, diving up to depths of 20 feet to catch fish.

Blue-footed boobies have a unique courtship ritual which involves the male raising his feet to show off his blue feet.

The female will then touch his feet with hers to show her approval.

Blue-footed boobies usually lay two eggs at a time.

They nest on the ground in colonies of up to thousands of birds.

They can live up to 30 years in the wild.

Both parents take turns incubating the eggs and raising the chicks.

They eat mainly small fish such as anchovies and sardines.

They have a distinctive call which sounds like a loud "caw".

Blue-footed boobies are very agile in the air and can make sharp turns.

They can fly up to speeds of 30 miles per hour.

They are excellent hunters, catching their prey in mid-air.

They also hunt by "treading" the water, which is when they rapidly paddle their feet to catch fish.

They often use the same nesting sites for generations.

They are monogamous, meaning they mate for life.

The male and female share in the responsibilities of raising the chicks.

The chicks fledge at around 12 weeks of age.

Blue-footed boobies have excellent eyesight, and can spot fish from far away.

They have a special air sac in their throat which helps them dive deeper.

They can dive up to depths of 70 feet.

They mainly feed during the day, but will also hunt at night if the conditions are right.

Blue-footed boobies have been known to live up to 50 years in captivity.

They can often be seen "sunbathing" on the beach.

They have a unique form of communication known as "billing", which involves pressing their beaks together.

Young chicks are often seen "play fighting" with each other.

They are highly social birds, and form large colonies.

59

Blue-footed boobies are a protected species in Ecuador.

## Conclusion

We hope you've enjoyed learning about the amazing blue-footed boobies of Ecuador. These fascinating birds have some amazing behaviors and adaptations that make them truly unique. So next time you're in Ecuador, why not take a trip to the beach and see if you can spot some of these beautiful birds in their natural habitat!

# Thank you for reading this book!

If you found this book helpful, I would be grateful if you would **post an honest review on Amazon** so this book can reach other supportive readers like you!

All you need to do is digitally flip to the back and leave your review. Or visit amazon.com/author/senseipauldavid click the correct book cover and click on the blue link next to the yellow stars that say, "customer reviews."

*As always...*

*It's a great day to be alive!*

# Share Our FREE eBooks Now!

kidsonearth.life

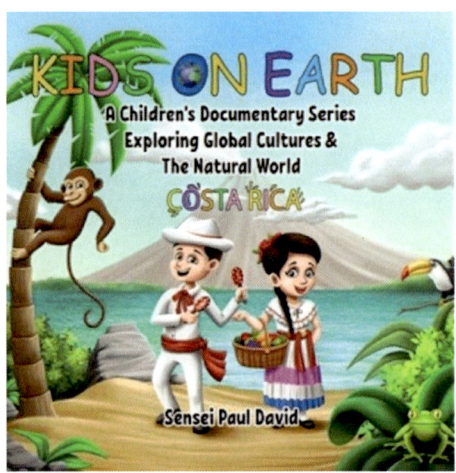

kidsonearth.world

# Click Below for Another Book In Each Series

senseipublishing.com/KoE_SERIES

senseipublishing.com/KoE_Wildlife_SERIES

## KoE En Español

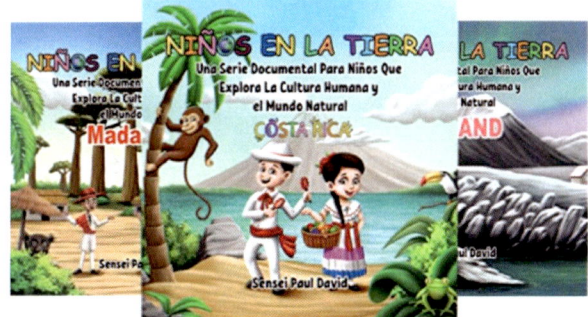

senseipublishing.com/KoE_SERIES_SPANISH

www.senseipublishing.com

Check out our **recommendations** for other books for adults & kids plus other great resources by visiting
www.senseipublishing.com/resources/

# Join Our Publishing Journey!

If you would like to receive FREE BOOKS and special offers, please visit www.senseipublishing.com and join our newsletter by entering your email address in the pop-up box

## Follow Our Engaging Blog NOW!
## senseipauldavid.ca

## Get Our FREE Books Today!

Click & Share the Links Below

### FREE Kids Books
lifeofbailey.senseipublishing.com
kidsonearth.senseipublishing.com

### FREE Self-Development Book

senseiselfdevelopment.senseipublishing.com

**FREE BONUS!!!**
**Experience Over 25 FREE Engaging Guided Meditations!**

Prized Skills & Practices for Adults & Kids. Help Restore Deep Sleep, Lower Stress, Improve Posture, Navigate Uncertainty & More.

Download the Free Insight Timer App and click the link below:
**http://insig.ht/sensei_paul**

# Thank you for reading this book!

If you found this book helpful, I would be grateful if you would **post an honest review on Amazon** so this book can reach other supportive readers like you!

All you need to do is digitally flip to the back and leave your review. Or visit amazon.com/author/senseipauldavid click the correct book cover and click on the blue link next to the yellow stars that say, "customer reviews."

*As always...*

*It's a great day to be alive!*

# Share Our FREE eBooks Now!

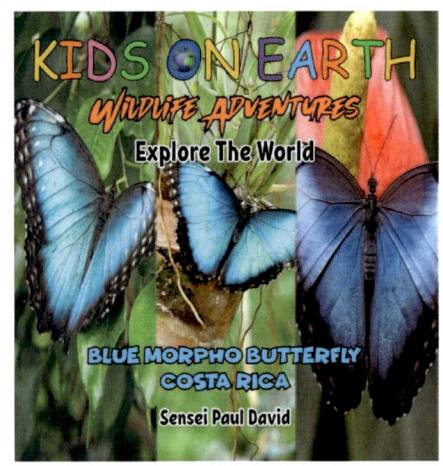

kidsonearth.life

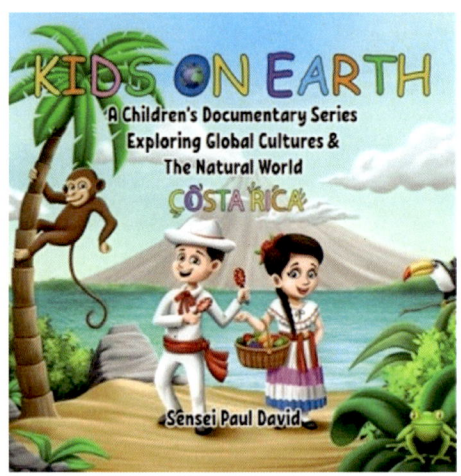

kidsonearth.world

# Thank you for reading this book!

If you found this book helpful, I would be grateful if you would **post an honest review on Amazon** so this book can reach other supportive readers like you!

All you need to do is digitally flip to the back and leave your review. Or visit amazon.com/author/senseipauldavid click the correct book cover and click on the blue link next to the yellow stars that say, "customer reviews."

*As always…*

*It's a great day to be alive!*

# Share Our FREE eBooks Now!

kidsonearth.life

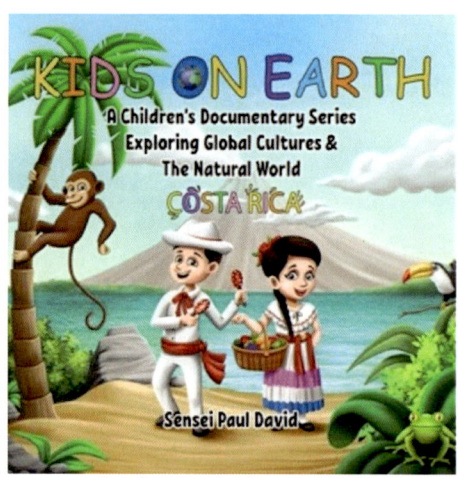

kidsonearth.world

The Kiel billed toucan is the national bird of Costa Rica.

# Introduction

Welcome to the wonderful world of toucans! Have you ever seen a toucan in real life? If so, you know how beautiful and fascinating these birds are. But did you know that the Kiel billed toucan is the national bird of Costa Rica? In this book, we will explore the Kiel billed toucan and thirty fun facts about them that you may not know. Through these facts, you will learn more about the Kiel billed toucan, its habitat, its diet, and its behavior. So let's get started!

# Join Our Publishing Journey!

If you would like to receive FUTURE FREE BOOKS and get to know us better, please click www.senseipublishing.com and join our newsletter by entering your email address in the pop-up box.

**Follow Our Blog: senseipauldavid.ca**

Follow/Like/Subscribe: Facebook, Instagram, YouTube: @senseipublishing

Scan the QR Code with your phone or tablet to follow us on social media:

Like / Subscribe / Follow

# Click Below for Another Book In Each Series

senseipublishing.com/KoE_SERIES     senseipublishing.com/KoE_Wildlife_SERIES

## KoE En Español

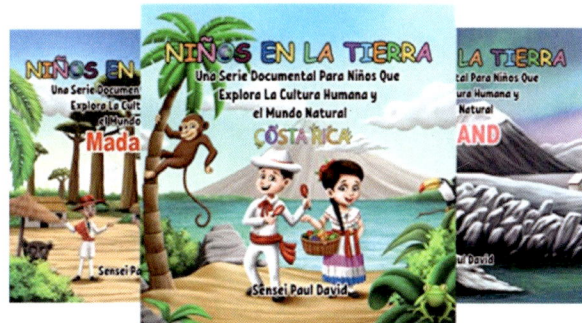

senseipublishing.com/KoE_SERIES_SPANISH

www.senseipublishing.com

# Get Our FREE Books Now!

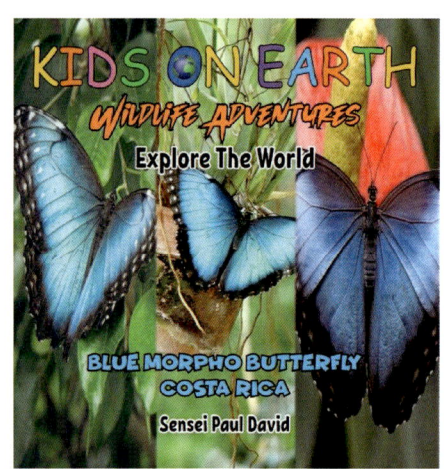

kidsonearth.life

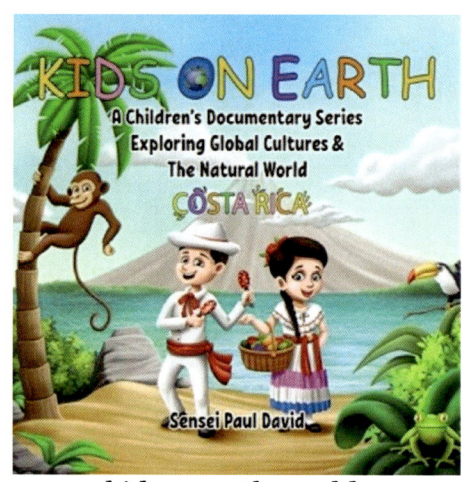

kidsonearth.world

# Synopsis

This book has provided an introduction to the Kiel Billed Toucan and the unique and fun facts about this amazing bird. Readers have learned about the Kiel Billed Toucan's habitat, diet, and behavior, as well as its importance to the rainforest. The Kiel Billed Toucan is a social species, often seen in small groups of up to 10 birds, and has a wide diet consisting of fruits, insects, lizards, and small birds. It is an important predator and seed disperser in the rainforest and has a wingspan of up to 3 feet and can reach speeds of up to 18 miles per hour in flight. The Kiel Billed Toucan is also an important pollinator and helps to spread the pollen of many different plants. We hope this book has been an enjoyable and informative read, and that readers have a better understanding of this incredible species.

# COPYRIGHT PAGE

Kids On Earth: Wildlife Adventures - Explore The World

Keel-Billed Toucan - Costa Rica

by Sensei Paul David,

Copyright © 2023.

All rights reserved.

978-1-77848-161-1 KoE_WildLife_Amazon_PaperbackBook_costarica_keel billed toucan

978-1-77848-160-4 KoE_WildLife_Amazon_eBook_costarica_keel billed toucan

978-1-77848-412-4 koe_wildlife_ingram_paperbackbook_keel billed toucan bird

This book is not authorized for free distribution copying.

www.senseipublishing.com

@senseipublishing
#senseipublishing

# KIDS ON EARTH

*Wildlife Adventures – Explore The World*

*Keel-Billed Toucan - Costa Rica*

Sensei Paul David

www.ingramcontent.com/pod-product-compliance
Lightning Source LLC
Chambersburg PA
CBRC090902080526
44587CB00008B/167

Scan & Follow/Like/Subscribe: Facebook, Instagram, YouTube: @senseipublishing

Scan using your phone/iPad camera for Social Media
Visit us at www.senseipublishing.com and sign up for our newsletter to learn more about our exciting books and to experience our FREE Guided Meditations for Kids & Adults.

# About the Author

I create simple & transformative eBooks & Guided Meditations for Adults & Children proven to help navigate uncertainty, solve niche problems & bring families closer together.

I'm a former finance project manager, private pilot, jiu-jitsu instructor, musician & former University of Toronto Fitness Trainer. I prefer a science-based approach to focus on these & other areas in my life to stay humble & hungry to evolve. I hope you enjoy my work and I'd love to hear your feedback.

- It's a great day to be alive!
Sensei Paul David

# About Sensei Publishing

Sensei Publishing commits itself to helping people of all ages transform into better versions of themselves by providing high-quality and research-based self-development books with an emphasis on mental health and guided meditations. Sensei Publishing offers well-written e-books, audiobooks, paperbacks, and online courses that simplify complicated but practical topics in line with its mission to inspire people toward positive transformation.

It's a great day to be alive!

**FREE BONUS!!!**
**Experience Over 25 FREE Engaging Guided Meditations!**

Prized Skills & Practices for Adults & Kids. Help Restore Deep Sleep, Lower Stress, Improve Posture, Navigate Uncertainty & More.

Download the Free Insight Timer App and click the link below:
**<u>http://insig.ht/sensei_paul</u>**

# Join Our Publishing Journey!

If you would like to receive FREE BOOKS and special offers, please visit www.senseipublishing.com and join our newsletter by entering your email address in the pop-up box

## Follow Our Engaging Blog NOW!
## senseipauldavid.ca

## Get Our FREE Books Today!

Click & Share the Links Below

### FREE Kids Books
lifeofbailey.senseipublishing.com
kidsonearth.senseipublishing.com

### FREE Self-Development Book

senseiselfdevelopment.senseipublishing.com

Check out our **recommendations** for other books for adults & kids plus other great resources by visiting
www.senseipublishing.com/resources/

# Click Below for Another Book In Each Series

senseipublishing.com/KoE_SERIES

senseipublishing.com/KoE_Wildlife_SERIES

## KoE En Español

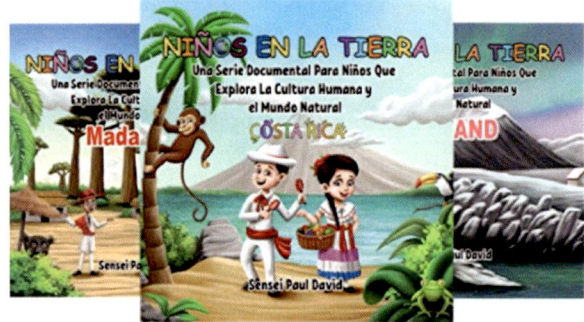

senseipublishing.com/KoE_SERIES_SPANISH

www.senseipublishing.com

The Kiel billed toucan makes its home in the tropical rainforests of Central and South America.

The Kiel billed toucan is the largest toucan species and can reach up to 24 inches in length.

The Kiel billed toucan is easily identified by its bright and multi-colored bill and feathers.

The Kiel billed toucan is an omnivore and will eat both plants and animals.

The Kiel billed toucan has a unique call that is a cross between a caw and a bark.

The Kiel billed toucan can live up to 25 years in the wild.

The Kiel billed toucan is often seen in pairs or small groups.

The Kiel billed toucan has a unique tongue that is longer than its bill.

The Kiel billed toucan is an excellent climber and can climb up to 20 feet in the air.

The Kiel billed toucan will use its bill to reach for fruit that is out of reach.

The Kiel billed toucan uses its bill to attract potential mates.

The Kiel billed toucan will build its nest in hollow tree trunks or branches.

The Kiel billed toucan is an important symbol of Costa Rican culture and heritage.

The Kiel billed toucan is a social bird and will often gather in large groups to feed.

The Kiel billed toucan is an important part of the forest ecosystem, helping to disperse seeds and maintain the balance of the forest.

The Kiel billed toucan is a vulnerable species, due to loss of habitat and poaching.

The Kiel billed toucan is a monogamous bird and will stay with the same mate for life.

The Kiel billed toucan is a popular animal in zoos and bird sanctuaries around the world.

The Kiel-billed toucan is a shy bird and will usually fly away when approached by humans.

The Kiel-billed toucan has been featured in several films and television shows.

The Kiel billed toucan is a very vocal bird and can be heard for miles.

The Kiel billed toucan has a very special diet, consisting of fruits, insects, lizards, and small birds.

The Kiel billed toucan is a very social bird and will often form large flocks when searching for food.

The Kiel billed toucan is a popular pet in some parts of the world.

The Kiel billed toucan is a very territorial bird and will defend its territory against other birds.

The Kiel billed toucan is an important symbol of Costa Rican tourism.

The Kiel billed toucan is an important part of the Costa Rican culture and is featured on the national flag and coins.

The Kiel billed toucan is an important part of the local economy, through tourism and conservation efforts.

The Kiel billed toucan is an important part of the Costa Rican identity and is considered a national treasure.

## Conclusion

Now that you've read these thirty fun facts about the Kiel billed toucan, you know just how amazing and important this bird is. From its bright yellow bill to its unique diet, the Kiel billed toucan is a fascinating and important part of Costa Rican culture. We hope that you have enjoyed learning about this beautiful bird and that you will help to protect it and its habitat.

# Thank you for reading this book!

If you found this book helpful, I would be grateful if you would **post an honest review on Amazon** so this book can reach other supportive readers like you!

All you need to do is digitally flip to the back and leave your review. Or visit amazon.com/author/senseipauldavid click the correct book cover and click on the blue link next to the yellow stars that say, "customer reviews."

*As always...*

*It's a great day to be alive!*

# Share Our FREE eBooks Now!

kidsonearth.life

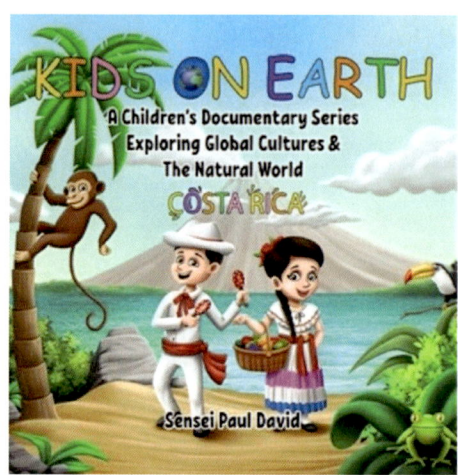

kidsonearth.world

# Click Below for Another Book In Each Series

senseipublishing.com/KoE_SERIES     senseipublishing.com/KoE_Wildlife_SERIES

## KoE En Español

senseipublishing.com/KoE_SERIES_SPANISH

www.senseipublishing.com

Check out our **recommendations** for other books for adults & kids plus other great resources by visiting
www.senseipublishing.com/resources/

# Join Our Publishing Journey!

If you would like to receive FREE BOOKS and special offers, please visit www.senseipublishing.com and join our newsletter by entering your email address in the pop-up box

## Follow Our Engaging Blog NOW!
## senseipauldavid.ca

## Get Our FREE Books Today!

Click & Share the Links Below

## FREE Kids Books

lifeofbailey.senseipublishing.com
kidsonearth.senseipublishing.com

## FREE Self-Development Book

senseiselfdevelopment.senseipublishing.com

## FREE BONUS!!!
## Experience Over 25 FREE Engaging Guided Meditations!

Prized Skills & Practices for Adults & Kids. Help Restore Deep Sleep, Lower Stress, Improve Posture, Navigate Uncertainty & More.

Download the Free Insight Timer App and click the link below:
**http://insig.ht/sensei_paul**

# About Sensei Publishing

Sensei Publishing commits itself to helping people of all ages transform into better versions of themselves by providing high-quality and research-based self-development books with an emphasis on mental health and guided meditations. Sensei Publishing offers well-written e-books, audiobooks, paperbacks, and online courses that simplify complicated but practical topics in line with its mission to inspire people toward positive transformation.

It's a great day to be alive!

# About the Author

I create simple & transformative eBooks & Guided Meditations for Adults & Children proven to help navigate uncertainty, solve niche problems & bring families closer together.

I'm a former finance project manager, private pilot, jiu-jitsu instructor, musician & former University of Toronto Fitness Trainer. I prefer a science-based approach to focus on these & other areas in my life to stay humble & hungry to evolve. I hope you enjoy my work and I'd love to hear your feedback.

- It's a great day to be alive!
Sensei Paul David

Scan & Follow/Like/Subscribe: Facebook, Instagram, YouTube: @senseipublishing

Scan using your phone/iPad camera for Social Media
Visit us at www.senseipublishing.com and sign up for our newsletter to learn more about our exciting books and to experience our FREE Guided Meditations for Kids & Adults.

www.ingramcontent.com/pod-product-compliance
Lightning Source LLC
Chambersburg PA
CBRC090902080526
44587CB00008B/168